Original title:
The Quiet Solstice

Copyright © 2024 Swan Charm
All rights reserved.

Author: Lan Donne
ISBN HARDBACK: 978-9916-79-507-1
ISBN PAPERBACK: 978-9916-79-508-8
ISBN EBOOK: 978-9916-79-509-5

Breath of a New Beginning

In the silence of the dawn,
Whispers ride the gentle breeze,
Hope awakens with the light,
Nature sings with perfect ease.

A tapestry of golden rays,
Weave through fingertips of dew,
Each moment holds a promise,
A chance to start anew.

The heart beats with sweet desire,
To shed the weight of yesterday,
Through trials faced, we rise inspired,
Onward to a brighter day.

Embrace the rhythm of the earth,
In every step, a dance of fate,
With courage blooming in our chests,
We forge ahead, create, create.

So breathe in deep, let worries fade,
The world unfolds with every breath,
In every end, a seed is sown,
For life is love, and love is life.

The Beauty of Waiting

In quiet moments, time stands still,
A gentle breath, a heart to fill.
With patience strong, the soul will grow,
In waiting's arms, the joys will flow.

The sun dips low, a golden hue,
Each passing hour, a dance that's true.
When dreams take shape in silent nights,
The beauty blooms in soft delights.

With stars that twinkle in the sky,
The world unfolds, a lullaby.
In tranquil hearts, the hopes ignite,
The beauty of waiting feels so right.

The breeze whispers secrets unheard,
In stillness found, a calming word.
Through every pause, a spark remains,
In beauty's grasp, we shed our chains.

So let us wait, embrace the time,
And in that space, our spirits climb.
For beauty lingers in the span,
Of every wish, of every plan.

Whispered Wishes at Dusk

As twilight falls, the world turns gold,
Soft whispers drift where stories unfold.
In shadows long, the hearts confide,
Wishes linger on the evening tide.

The sky ignites with hues of blush,
Each heartbeat echoes, the softest hush.
In fading light, we find our way,
Whispered wishes at the end of day.

The stars awaken with dreams to share,
In gentle breezes, we breathe the air.
With open hearts, we seek and find,
Whispered hopes entwined in kind.

Under the blanket of starlit skies,
Every wish painted with sighs.
The universe listens, it understands,
Our whispered dreams rest in its hands.

The dusk invites us to dream anew,
In silent prayers, our hopes accrue.
For in that moment, all feels right,
Whispered wishes take their flight.

Soft Light of Stillness

In the morning calm, the world awakes,
Soft light spills in, the silence breaks.
Each ray a promise of peace ahead,
In stillness found, our worries shed.

The gentle breeze caresses the trees,
Awakening life, a soothing tease.
With open hearts, we breathe in deep,
In soft light's grasp, our troubles sleep.

Time slows down, a precious gift,
In quiet moments, we find our lift.
With nature's brush, our spirits mend,
Soft light of stillness, a perfect blend.

The colors dance on the canvas wide,
In harmony, our hearts abide.
Each flicker of light, a guiding star,
So close to peace, we've come so far.

In every heartbeat, a soft refrain,
The calmness found, a sweet sustain.
In stillness, we find our way to be,
With soft light's grace, we feel so free.

Night's Secret Garden

Beneath the stars, a garden waits,
With secrets held behind dark gates.
The moonlight spills, a silver stream,
In night's embrace, we softly dream.

The flowers whisper in the night,
Each petal glows with gentle light.
In shadows deep, their magic glows,
Night's secret garden softly flows.

With every step, a fragrance swirls,
In hidden paths, the mystery unfurls.
As crickets sing their serenade,
In twilight's arms, our worries fade.

The night reveals what day conceals,
In secret blooms, the heart reveals.
With stars as lanterns up above,
This garden breathes with quiet love.

So linger here, let time suspend,
In night's embrace, let spirits blend.
For in this space, our dreams take flight,
In night's secret garden, all feels right.

Lanterns of Solace

In the stillness of night,
Lanterns glow so bright,
Whispers of the past,
Shadows fading fast.

Memories softly weave,
Through the hearts that grieve,
Guiding gentle hands,
To forgotten lands.

Each flicker a story,
Of lost love and glory,
Light leads the way home,
Where no soul must roam.

Underneath the stars,
Healing unseen scars,
Lanterns lift the veil,
Of dreams that prevail.

In the warmth they bring,
Hope starts to sing,
In the quiet space,
Finding our own grace.

Echoes of the Dark

In shadows deep and wide,
Where secrets tend to bide,
Echoes whisper low,
Of things we don't know.

The night holds its breath,
In silence, it is death,
Yet in the stillness, sound,
Of lost souls unbound.

Winds carry the cries,
Of those who flew too high,
Through the trees they creep,
Veiled in twilight's keep.

Footsteps softly roam,
In a world far from home,
The dark sings a tune,
Beneath a waning moon.

Hope flickers and fades,
As the darkness parades,
In the night's embrace,
We search for a trace.

Whispering Moonlight

Moonlight dances soft,
Whispers float aloft,
Glistening on the sea,
Telling tales to me.

Each beam a gentle kiss,
In the dark, a bliss,
Inviting dreams to play,
As night turns to day.

Stars join the refrain,
In a silvery chain,
Guided by the light,
Chasing off the night.

All secrets held tight,
Come alive in flight,
Underneath the glow,
Hopes begin to flow.

With every sighing breeze,
The heart learns to ease,
In this sacred space,
Find our quiet grace.

Veiled in Solitude

Beneath the heavy shroud,
Of silence, calm and proud,
Solitude becomes friend,
As worries start to mend.

In stillness, thoughts arise,
Like whispers from the skies,
Each moment a chance,
To reflect and dance.

Veiled in quiet hues,
Infinite shades we choose,
The heart starts to see,
What it yearns to be.

In the depths, we explore,
Rich treasures evermore,
Finding strength within,
Where our souls begin.

Let the silence guide,
With nothing to hide,
In solitude's embrace,
We uncover grace.

Murmurs of the Silent Woods

In the stillness where shadows creep,
Whispers of the night softly seep.
Beneath the branches, secrets lie,
With every rustle, a gentle sigh.

Moonlight dances on leaves of green,
Stars peek down, a tranquil scene.
The heart of nature, calm and wise,
Amidst the trees, the spirit flies.

Echoes of footsteps, lost in time,
Nature's symphony, a silent rhyme.
Each stirring breeze tells a tale,
Of wanderers' hearts and the paths they trail.

Deer pause in glades, in quiet grace,
A fleeting moment, a sacred space.
In the depths of the woods, we find,
The murmurs of peace that soothe the mind.

As dawn approaches, colors burst,
Waking the world from dreams rehearsed.
In the silent woods, life finds a way,
A sacred promise of a new day.

Frost-Laden Serenity

Upon the ground, a blanket white,
Nature rests in tranquil flight.
Sparkling crystals shimmer bright,
In the quiet of the winter's night.

Trees adorned with icy lace,
Every branch, a frozen grace.
Silent whispers in the air,
Frost-laden beauty, beyond compare.

Footsteps crunch on snowy trails,
A breath of magic where stillness prevails.
Beneath the stars so deeply set,
A world transformed, densely met.

Warmth within a chill so grand,
The heart finds peace, a soft hand.
Time stands still in this embrace,
Wrapped in winter's gentle face.

As dawn's light kisses the frost,
In quiet moments, nothing's lost.
Frost-laden serenity fills the heart,
A winter's gift, a work of art.

The Breath of a Winter's Night

In the hush of a frosty eve,
Stars like diamonds begin to weave.
Whispers of winter fill the air,
A story told with utmost care.

Snowflakes fall, a gentle shower,
Each one unique, a fleeting flower.
Nature's breath, both soft and cold,
A silent secret waiting to be told.

Moonlight glimmers on the snow,
Shadows dance, putting on a show.
In the stillness, hearts align,
As the night unfolds, pure and divine.

Each chilly wind, a soft caress,
Filling souls with peacefulness.
Wrapped in blankets of crystal light,
We find our place in winter's night.

The world asleep, a blanket deep,
Dreams wander where silence keeps.
The breath of winter, calm and bright,
Guides us softly into the night.

Lanterns of the Frostbound Sky

Gaze above where wonders flow,
Lanterns of frost begin to glow.
Stars ignite the velvet night,
A canvas stitched with purest light.

In the chill, the world ignites,
Frozen wonders take their flights.
Each twinkle tells a loving tale,
Of dreams that soar on a breathy gale.

Underneath the vast expanse,
Whispers linger, shadows dance.
In the dark, hope's warmth will rise,
Carried by the frostbound skies.

With every breath, the night unfolds,
Mysteries wrapped in silvers and golds.
Lanterns of life, forever bright,
Illuminate the depths of night.

As dawn approaches, softness spreads,
Leaving traces upon our beds.
Frostbound skies, where dreams align,
In their embrace, our spirits shine.

Whispers of Dusk

As day retreats from the sky,
Soft whispers weave through the trees.
Crimson hues begin to die,
In twilight's tender breeze.

Stars awaken one by one,
The moon glows with silver light.
As shadows dance, the day is done,
The world sighs into night.

Quiet moments gather close,
Nature's lullaby unfolds.
The heart finds peace, a gentle dose,
In dusk's embrace, the soul holds.

Fading echoes drift away,
As dreams take flight in the dark.
In the stillness, emotions sway,
Guided by a haunting spark.

Forever holds the dusk's sweet song,
A tender end to every day.
In whispers soft, we all belong,
As night unfolds, we lose our way.

Shadows of the Longest Night

Beneath the veil of starlit skies,
A quiet hush blankets the land.
In shadows deep, the stillness lies,
Dreams gather, hand in hand.

Time slows down in this embrace,
Where darkness holds its silent sway.
Each heartbeat echoes a hidden grace,
As night embraces the day.

Whispers of ghosts from long ago,
Drift along the chilling air.
In the depths where memories flow,
Every secret laid bare.

The moon cloaked in shadows dense,
Keeps watch over the sleeping town.
In her light, a mystic fence,
Hides the fears that abound.

In the longest night, we find our truth,
A moment to reflect and pause.
In the stillness, the soul's sweet proof,
A dance with the night, a silent applause.

Stillness in the Hollow

In the hollow where silence reigns,
Whispers of winds softly sigh.
Nature speaks in muted strains,
As twilight begins to lie.

Each leaf holds a story untold,
Of seasons past, of time's embrace.
In the stillness, memories unfold,
In every shadow, a trace.

Moss-covered stones grace the ground,
As soft feet tread where echoes sleep.
Through the calm, peace can be found,
In the hollow, the heart takes a leap.

Clouds gather, casting a shroud,
Yet sparks of light peek through the gray.
In the hollow, life is proud,
Embracing night, welcoming day.

In this stillness, let thoughts drift,
Like feathers floating from above.
In the hollow, a gentle gift,
Whispers of nature, steeped in love.

Echoes of Frosted Pines

In the forest where pines stand tall,
Frost embraces every limb.
Whispers of winter softly call,
In the quiet, life feels dim.

Each branch adorned in crystal white,
Casts shadows on the frozen ground.
Underneath the pale moonlight,
Secrets of the woods abound.

Footsteps crunch in the silent space,
As echoes dance on frosty air.
In this realm of serene grace,
Every breath becomes a prayer.

Time moves slow through the chilly night,
As stars twinkle in a velvet sea.
Beneath the cloak of silver light,
Nature whispers, wild and free.

In the pines, where the whispers play,
A symphony of quiet cheer.
Through the frost, we find our way,
Echoes of magic, always near.

Silent Shadows at Dusk

Whispers weave through the trees,
Casting shapes that dance with ease.
In the hush, secrets unfold,
Silent shadows, stories told.

Moonlight glimmers on the lake,
A gentle breeze, the lilies quake.
Night unveils a velvet shroud,
As day sighs out, soft and proud.

Crickets sing their evening song,
Nature's choir, where we belong.
Stars ignite the evening sky,
Silent shadows, a soft sigh.

Fading light begins to steal,
A tranquil world, the heart can feel.
Time slows down, the moments pause,
In this realm, there are no flaws.

Let the night embrace your soul,
In its depths, you can be whole.
Silent shadows cradle dreams,
In the dark, the magic gleams.

When Day Meets Night

Golden hues begin to fade,
As twilight's curtain starts its trade.
The horizon tinged with red,
Bringing forth the night ahead.

Birds retreat to nests of rest,
While crickets hum their evening best.
The sun bows low with tired eyes,
A soft farewell to summer skies.

Coolness wraps the world in grace,
As stars emerge to take their place.
Day's adventures slipping past,
Wrapped in night's serene contrast.

Shadows stretch and gently merge,
In the stillness, hearts converge.
With every breath, we find the peace,
When day meets night, our worries cease.

So let the nightfall sing its song,
In this embrace, we all belong.
Together in the twilight's embrace,
When day meets night, we find our space.

Solstice Serenade

The longest day, a golden thread,
Where ancient songs of light are spread.
In the warmth, we bask and play,
As summer blooms, it lights our way.

Fields adorned in vibrant hues,
Nature dances, spreading news.
Underneath the blooming trees,
Joyful laughter on the breeze.

Sun-kissed moments slowly wane,
As twilight's brush softens the pain.
The longest night begins to creep,
In the solace, dreams run deep.

Whispers of the seasons' change,
Embrace their rhythm, feel the range.
From meadows bright to starlit skies,
Solstice serenades arise.

So gather near, let spirits soar,
In this magic, we want more.
Each note we sing, a bond we share,
In harmony, we conquer care.

Hushed Harmonies of the Year

Seasons turn, a gentle grace,
In each moment, find your place.
Winter whispers, summer sings,
Hushed harmonies of life's strings.

In spring's cradle, blooms awake,
A tapestry that nature makes.
Colors burst, the world ignites,
In the calm of golden nights.

Summer's warmth, a sunlit dance,
Inviting all to take a chance.
In late evenings, shadows play,
As dusk brings forth a soft ballet.

Autumn leaves, a rustling sound,
Painting paths upon the ground.
A cycle woven, old yet new,
In every breath, life's hues accrue.

Each season holds a story clear,
In time's embrace, we persevere.
Hushed harmonies, an endless flow,
In nature's symphony, we grow.

The Year's Gentle Farewell

The leaves drift softly down,
Whispers of a time well spent.
Colors fade into the ground,
A moment to reflect, content.

The days have danced and twirled,
Each sunset kissed our skies.
Now the night unfurls,
With stars that softly rise.

Memories held close and dear,
In shadows of the past.
A hint of joy, a trace of fear,
In this moment, we hold fast.

Quiet laughter fills the air,
As friends gather for a toast.
Let's savor joy, lay bare,
The moments we cherish most.

With humble hearts, we say goodbye,
To a year that shaped our souls.
In its embrace, we learned to fly,
Now we step towards new goals.

Serene Flickers of Light

In the stillness of the night,
Stars begin to softly glow.
A gentle breeze takes flight,
Whispers of the earth below.

Candles flicker, casting dreams,
Upon the walls, a dance of shade.
In silence, of thoughts and themes,
The quiet moments generously made.

Each dawn brings a new hue,
Colors blending, bright and soft.
Hope emerges, pure and true,
As daylight lifts our hearts aloft.

In the garden, shadows play,
Innocence in petals wide.
Nature sings, in bright array,
Where all of life's secrets hide.

As evening falls, we find our peace,
Serene reflections in our sight.
In these moments, worries cease,
Capturing flickers of light.

Hushed Revelations

In whispers of the autumn breeze,
Secrets linger, soft and low.
Stories told beneath the trees,
Where gentle hearts can learn to grow.

Each sigh a touch of grace,
In twilight's tender embrace.
The world slows down its gait,
In hushed tones, we contemplate.

A single leaf falls to the ground,
Lessons woven in its flight.
In silence, we can be unbound,
Finding truth in shadows' light.

The stars above, a guiding hand,
As dreams awaken in the night.
Together, we will stand,
In trust, we find our way to light.

With every heartbeat, wisdom comes,
In stillness, questions fade away.
In peaceful moments, truth becomes,
The whispers of the end of day.

Secrets of a Quiet Hour

In a still room, the world fades,
Time pauses, a gentle sigh.
Thoughts linger in hidden glades,
As moments drift softly by.

Books unopened on the shelf,
Pages waiting for a glance.
In silence, we find ourselves,
Wrapped in this still expanse.

Outside, the moon takes her throne,
Casting silver on the floor.
In the quiet, we are alone,
Yet within, we feel much more.

The clock ticks softly, marking time,
Each second a heartbeat's grace.
In peace, we may find a rhyme,
Lost in this sacred space.

Secrets whispered on the breeze,
In shadows of a deeper hour.
In silence, every heart agrees,
There is beauty in this power.

Twilight's Peace

Sunset hues paint the sky,
Whispers of the day goodbye.
Stars begin to softly gleam,
Nature settles, like a dream.

Night's embrace, soft and warm,
Crisp air stirs, a gentle charm.
Quiet moments fill the air,
Breathe in peace, free from care.

Crickets sing their evening song,
Nature's chorus, sweet and strong.
Moonlight dances on the ground,
In this stillness, calm is found.

Time slows down, the world feels right,
Underneath the soothing night.
Each breath lingers, life is slow,
In twilight's peace, let worries go.

Embrace the dark, let go of light,
In twilight's arms, hold on tight.
Feel the magic, sense the grace,
Find your heart's most quiet place.

Reflections in the Twilight

Golden rays fade from sight,
Mirrored in the calm of night.
Clouds drift slowly, shadows play,
Whispers linger, dreams convey.

Rippling water, still and clear,
Echoes of the day draw near.
Thoughts like ripples form and fade,
Lost in hues that nature made.

Overhead, the stars ignite,
Guiding minds with gentle light.
Reflections dance upon the sea,
In this moment, just be free.

From the depth of twilight's gaze,
Find your thoughts in evening's haze.
Nature's canvas, soft and wide,
Shows a place where hearts abide.

In the twilight, dreams will soar,
While the world waits at the door.
Trust the silence, feel the tune,
In this space, feel the moon.

The Calm Between

In the hush of dawn's embrace,
Find the stillness, find your place.
Gentle whispers, hush the day,
In this calm, let worries sway.

Life's a dance, both fast and slow,
In between, let patience grow.
Moments linger, softly pause,
In between, find hidden laws.

Storms may rage, the skies may cry,
Still, there's calm before goodbye.
Breathe it in, this sacred space,
In the pause, you find your grace.

As the sun begins to rise,
Feel the peace in soft replies.
Hearts will find their gentle beat,
In the calm, they find retreat.

Every moment, every breath,
In between, we conquer death.
Hold the silence, share the song,
In the calm, we all belong.

Softening Shadows

As the sun melts into night,
Shadows soften, lose their fight.
Gentle hues embrace the sky,
A tender sigh as day says bye.

Branches sway in whispered breeze,
Nighttime's kiss brings sweet unease.
Chill of air, soft touch of light,
Paints the world in shades of night.

Footsteps hush, the earth holds still,
As the heart begins to thrill.
Feel the magic wrap around,
In the dusk, a tranquil sound.

Stars awaken, shyly peep,
In their glow, the shadows creep.
Quiet moments, time to rest,
In softening shadows, feel blessed.

Days may fade, but dreams endure,
In this twilight, love is pure.
Embrace the night, let worries cease,
In softening shadows, find your peace.

Silence Amidst the Stars

In the stillness of the night,
Whispers dance with silver light.
Each twinkle tells a tale so grand,
As shadows softly weave the strand.

The moon hangs low with gentle grace,
Casting dreams across the space.
Yet in this quiet, hearts expand,
Finding peace where thoughts can land.

With every breath, the cosmos sighs,
Echoes mingle with starry skies.
Infinite wonders, vast and bright,
Guarded secrets in the night.

Time slows down, the world fades away,
Wrapped in warmth where feelings play.
In solitude, we find our way,
Reaching out to gentle sway.

A silent wish on starlight's beam,
In this haven, we dare to dream.
Amongst the stars, we learn to fly,
In silence, we touch the sky.

Veil of the Evening Sky

The sun dips low, the day must rest,
A canvas painted, nature's best.
Crimson hues in twilight's glance,
The world prepares for night's slow dance.

As shadows elongate in the glow,
Soft winds carry whispers low.
Underneath the vast expanse,
The evening sings a sweet romance.

Stars awaken, shy and bright,
Like little gems in the soft night.
They sparkle, twinkle, softly sway,
A mystical game where dreams play.

A veil of night drapes calm and cool,
In this space, the heart can schools.
Moments linger, hopes arise,
Lost and found beneath the skies.

Beneath this shroud of twilight's grace,
Finding solace in a hidden place.
In the quiet, the spirit glows,
As the night's serene beauty flows.

A Moment of Starlight

Caught in a breathless, fleeting glance,
A moment's magic, a cosmic dance.
Stars align in the velvet night,
Igniting hearts with pure delight.

Beneath the heavens, wishes soar,
Every glimmer opens a door.
In stillness, dreams begin to rise,
Carried high under sprawling skies.

Timeless echoes in the quiet air,
Lifting souls without a care.
For in that instant, all is clear,
A gentle peace, the stars draw near.

Through the dark, a light ignites,
Guiding lost souls to enchanting heights.
A whisper soft, a secret shared,
In the starlight, love declared.

Hold this moment, let it seep,
Into the heart where feelings keep.
A single glance, a timeless spark,
A dance of joy within the dark.

Fragments of Solitude

In fragments scattered, silence speaks,
A gentle echo through the peaks.
Whispers linger in the air,
Carrying burdens, light as care.

Each moment stretched, a breath sublime,
Caught in the folds of fleeting time.
Shadows play upon the ground,
In solitude, the soul is found.

Reflections dance in the moonlight,
Crafting stories in the night.
Within the quiet, thoughts unite,
Weaving solace into sight.

Embraced by night's gentle shroud,
Wrapped in whispers, soft and loud.
Pieces merge, the heart aligns,
In solitude, the spirit shines.

Fragments gather, forming whole,
Filling spaces in the soul.
In the stillness, we intertwine,
Finding peace, the stars align.

The Embrace of Darkened Sun

Beneath the veil of twilight glow,
Shadows stretch, where soft winds blow.
Whispers dance in muted light,
A fleeting kiss of day and night.

Echoes of the sun's last breath,
Wrap the world in shades of death.
Colors blend in subtle haze,
As daylight fades in smoky maze.

Figures linger in dusky fields,
Where silence blooms, and stillness yields.
The sky adorned with obsidian,
A somber hymn, a darkened pin.

Hands reach out to touch the void,
In shadows deep, the heart's deployed.
Each moment trapped in fleeting time,
Resonates a haunting chime.

What lives beyond the grasp of day,
Our fears converge where spirits sway.
In the embrace, we find our place,
The darkened sun, a soft embrace.

In the Stillness of Falling Snow

Softly drifts the winter's grace,
Blanketing all in gentle embrace.
Whispers float on frosted air,
As time suspends in icy glare.

Branches bow with heavy crowns,
Silence blankets this sleepy town.
Footprints vanish, lost in white,
Nature's peace, a pure delight.

Each flake tells a tale of cold,
In stillness, secrets yet untold.
Stars peek through the velvet night,
Softly guiding with their light.

The world transforms in softest hue,
Every heartbeat feels brand new.
Moments linger, warm yet shy,
As snowflakes fall from twilight sky.

In the hush of winter's call,
We find the strength to stand tall.
In the stillness, hearts awake,
In love's warmth, the cold we shake.

Gentle Shadows of Evening

The sun retreats, the horizon glows,
As twilight weaves through softest prose.
Shadows stretch across the lawn,
Brush the world before the dawn.

Whispers in the fading light,
Carry hopes in gentle flight.
Stars prepare to take their throne,
In the quiet, we're not alone.

Branches sway with whispered dreams,
Flow like water, dance in streams.
The night's embrace is drawing near,
In the silence, we find our cheer.

Moonbeams play on petals soft,
In their glow, we lift aloft.
Every shadow tells a story,
Of fleeting love and faded glory.

Gentle dusk paints skies in gray,
As day surrenders to night's sway.
In shadows, life begins to blend,
Evening whispers never end.

Murmurs of an Icy Dawn

Crystals shimmer on the ground,
Morning whispers make no sound.
Breath like smoke in crisp, cool air,
Promises hang, everywhere.

A world anew, untouched by time,
Every step feels like a rhyme.
Nature stirs in frosted dreams,
Awakening where beauty gleams.

Birds take flight on silent wings,
Echo through the chilly rings.
Light creeps in with golden hue,
Painting landscapes, fresh and new.

The icy dawn, a sacred space,
Glimmers softly, warms the face.
In the stillness, hearts will yearn,
For the warmth of day's return.

Murmurs weave in morning's light,
As shadows flee from the night.
In every breath, a promise found,
In the peace of icy ground.

The Call of the Winter Moon

In the night, the moon shines bright,
Casting shadows, a silver light.
Whispers travel through the trees,
Calling forth the winter breeze.

Stars awaken in the dark,
Awed by beauty, leaving a mark.
Snowflakes dance in chilly air,
Spinning tales without a care.

Silence wraps the world in peace,
Pillowed dreams never cease.
Nature holds its breath tonight,
Underneath the moon's soft light.

The call of winter, calm and deep,
In the sphere where secrets sleep.
Echoes of a frosty song,
Linger on for nights so long.

As the world finds its own tune,
Beneath the watchful winter moon.
Each moment sows a tender thread,
In dreams where warmth will soon be spread.

Embraced by Frost

Morning breaks in icy lace,
Nature dons a crystal face.
Trees stand dressed in white delight,
Embraced by frost, a stunning sight.

Birds take flight with wings so bold,
Chasing sun, the warmth they hold.
Yet in stillness, hearts reside,
In the chill, no need to hide.

Shivers dance upon the ground,
As a silence wraps around.
Life prepares for springtime's kiss,
In each frosty breath, such bliss.

Moments hold their fleeting grace,
In the winter's soft embrace.
Time stands still, a pause so sweet,
In the cycle, life's heartbeat.

Here we find a time to grow,
In the cold, the heart can glow.
Frosted dreams beneath the sky,
Await the warmth, the sun's soft sigh.

The Calm Before the Dawn

Beneath the shroud of quiet night,
A world asleep, devoid of light.
Stars begin their fading glow,
As time prepares for morning's show.

Whispers thread the gentle air,
Softly weaving dreams to share.
Crickets hum their lullabies,
While shadows stretch and slowly rise.

The horizon starts to gleam,
Painting o'er the midnight dream.
Colors blend in soft embrace,
As night yields to daylight's grace.

Echoes of the midnight song,
Fade as dawn begins to throng.
In this pause, the world awaits,
Opening to morning's gates.

A heartbeat waits, a breath is drawn,
In the calm before the dawn.
Time holds still, a gentle sigh,
As hope unfolds beneath the sky.

Hibernating Whispers

In the woods where shadows play,
Creatures rest and hide away.
Leaves turn crisp beneath their feet,
Hibernating, they find retreat.

Drifting into dreamscape realms,
Time quietly overwhelms.
Nature's pulse begins to slow,
As frosty winds begin to blow.

Whispers echo through the trees,
Telling tales on chilly breeze.
In the stillness, life resides,
While the chilly secret hides.

Underneath the snow's embrace,
Life prepares in hidden space.
Seeds of spring are waiting near,
In the calm, they persevere.

And when the sun begins to rise,
Shaking off its slumbered guise,
Hibernating whispers bloom,
Bringing life back from the gloom.

Still Waters at Dawn

Morning light breaks soft and clear,
Reflections whisper, calm and near.
Birds awaken, softly sing,
A new day stirs, life taking wing.

Shadows dance on tranquil streams,
Nature's peace weaves silent dreams.
Gentle ripples kiss the shore,
Stillness holds us, wanting more.

Colors blend in pastel hues,
The world awakens, fresh with views.
Beneath the surface, secrets lay,
In still waters, hopes at play.

Time slows down, a breath we take,
Each moment holds a chance to wake.
Dawn's embrace, a sweet caress,
In quietude, we find our rest.

As sun ascends, the day begins,
With every heartbeat, life's sweet spins.
Still waters reflect the sky's grace,
In silence, we find our place.

The Calm in the Chaos

Amidst the noise, a breath, a pause,
Finding peace without a cause.
The world spins fast, yet here I stand,
In quiet moments, life feels grand.

Rushing waters, wild and free,
In the storm, a part of me.
Between the waves, a steady heart,
In the chaos, I am art.

Voices clash, a storm of sound,
But deep within, I'm safe and bound.
A sanctuary in my mind,
In this madness, solace find.

Time cascades like falling leaves,
In every breath, the soul believes.
The calm emerges, strength anew,
In trouble's midst, I blossom too.

Through the noise, I hear my song,
A soft reminder, I belong.
Amidst the chaos, hear the call,
In stillness, I can conquer all.

Luminous Echoes

Stars alight in velvet skies,
Whispers dance in moonlit sighs.
Each spark a tale, a faded dream,
In night's embrace, soft glimmers beam.

Shadows stretch, the world held tight,
Echoes shimmer, soft and bright.
Through the dark, a glimmer glows,
A silent song that softly flows.

Timeless songs of ages past,
In every echo, spirit cast.
A rhythm sways through night's cool breath,
In luminous whispers, life and death.

Feel the vastness of the night,
In its heart, a spark of light.
Every moment is a song,
Luminous echoes, where we belong.

As stars fade with the break of dawn,
Let dreams linger, gently drawn.
In the silence, find your way,
Through luminous echoes, night meets day.

Chords of a Silent Night

Glistening stars in the deep, dark vault,
The world wrapped in quiet, without fault.
Underneath the blanket of endless night,
Soft chords resonate, pure delight.

A gentle breeze hums through the trees,
Carrying whispers with tender ease.
Moonbeams trace on sleeping land,
In silence, beauty takes a stand.

Each moment holds a soft refrain,
In stillness, we release our pain.
Harmony flows through the cool night air,
Chords of peace, a moment rare.

The heartbeats echo, slow and deep,
In the vastness, secrets keep.
As dreams drift on the midnight tide,
We find solace, hearts open wide.

Chords of a night, serene and bright,
In the quiet, we ignite.
With every breath, we weave our song,
In silent reverie, we belong.

Time's Gentle Suspension

In a moment, we linger slow,
The clock's hands weave a soft glow.
Gentle whispers fill the air,
As time holds still, beyond compare.

Memories dance in twilight's hue,
A tapestry, woven anew.
The world outside fades to grey,
While inside, we choose to stay.

In this instant, hearts align,
As shadows stretch, we intertwine.
The past and future softly blend,
In time's embrace, there's no end.

Moments splash like colors bright,
A canvas painted with pure delight.
In gentle pauses, we find grace,
A precious, fleeting, sacred space.

With each tick, the silence sings,
Of love and hope, of simple things.
In time's gentle suspension's grasp,
We find the joy that we can clasp.

Essence of the Night

Beneath the stars, the world feels light,
Whispers travel through the night.
Moonlit paths beckon the soul,
In shadows deep, we feel whole.

Crickets serenade the moon,
Echoes of a distant tune.
Each breeze carries soft delight,
The essence blooms in the night.

Misty dreams in silver beams,
Awake the heart with tender schemes.
In twilight's hush, uncertainty fades,
In the stillness, hope cascades.

Time drifts onward, yet we remain,
Caught in the thrill, free from pain.
As stars whisper secrets plain,
In this dark, we find our reign.

With the dawn, stories unfold,
The essence bright, the night's gold.
In every heart, a lingering spark,
Of the cherished dreams that light the dark.

Solstice's Gentle Brief

In the moment where shadows play,
The solstice brings a fleeting day.
A golden light, sharp yet sweet,
Where day and night gracefully meet.

The sun dips low, the sky ablaze,
In vibrant hues, the world does gaze.
With gentle warmth, the day retreats,
As the twilight softly meets.

Each breath a gift, each moment rare,
In the golden glow, we share.
With whispers of what's yet to come,
In solstice charm, the heartbeats hum.

The dance of seasons, brief and bright,
Calls us to hold the day's light tight.
In every heartbeat, hopes arise,
As day surrenders to starlit skies.

In harmony, the dusk unfolds,
In brief embrace, the warmth enfolds.
A fleeting glance of summer's kiss,
In solstice glow, we find our bliss.

Shadows of Anticipation

In the twilight, dreams take flight,
Filling the void with pure delight.
Each shadow holds a secret sound,
In the waiting, love is found.

The heartbeat of the fading day,
Whispers what the stars might say.
In silence, hope begins to bloom,
As life stirs gently in the gloom.

Anticipation weaves its thread,
Linking dreams yet to be tread.
With every breath, an urge to soar,
In shadows deep, we crave for more.

Laughter mingles with heartfelt sighs,
As the universe begins to rise.
A tapestry of wishes bright,
Woven in the shades of night.

With each moment, we draw near,
In the darkness, we feel no fear.
Embrace the whispers, soft and low,
For in anticipation, love will grow.

Between Fire and Frost

In whispers low, the embers glow,
A dance of warmth and icy flow.
Hearts entwined in nature's game,
Passions rise, yet cool the flame.

Through branches bare, the chill will creep,
While flames of dusk begin to leap.
The earth, it trembles, takes a breath,
Where life and silence flirt with death.

Softly melts the frost so bright,
In colors bold, the day turns night.
A moment caught, forever chased,
Between the fire and frost embraced.

With every spark, a bitter chill,
Life's balance, poised, a fragile thrill.
Echoes linger, shadows cast,
Where passions bloom, then fade so fast.

Let the seasons swirl and sway,
In this realm of night and day.
The dance of contrast, pure delight,
Forever bound, between fire and frost's light.

Nature's Quiet Respite

Among the trees, where silence reigns,
A gentle whisper, soft refrains.
The birds take flight, the leaves do sway,
In nature's arms, we drift away.

Beneath the boughs, a soft embrace,
Time stands still in this sacred space.
The sun peeks through, a golden ray,
A tender kiss to greet the day.

Water flows, a soothing song,
In nature's heart, where we belong.
With every breath, we taste the calm,
A healing balm, a peaceful psalm.

The flowers bloom, a vibrant hue,
Their fragrance sweet, as love feels true.
In every petal, life unfolds,
A quiet tale, through nature told.

As twilight falls, the stars appear,
In stillness found, we hold them dear.
Each moment savored, time at rest,
In nature's quiet, we are blessed.

The Ease of Shadows

As daylight fades, the shadows creep,
In twilight's grasp, we drift to sleep.
With muted colors, softly cast,
The past and future, tied and fast.

The world transformed, a cloak of night,
Whispers echo, soft and light.
In cool embrace, we find our peace,
The burdened heart begins release.

Beneath the stars, our dreams take flight,
In shadows' arms, we find our sight.
A hidden path, where secrets hide,
In quietude, our thoughts abide.

Every flicker, every sound,
A gentle pulse beneath the ground.
The ease of shadows, sweet and low,
A mirror to the soul's true glow.

From dusk to dawn, the journey flows,
Through every joy, through every woes.
We learn to dance in shades and tone,
In shadows' grace, we're never alone.

Embrace of the Fading Light

When sun dips low, the colors bleed,
In skies of gold, our hearts are freed.
The day gives way to twilight's sigh,
In this embrace, we learn to fly.

As shadows stretch, the world grows vast,
Each moment cherished, never past.
The gentle hues, they softly blend,
In fading light, we find a friend.

With every heartbeat, warmth remains,
A fleeting touch, like summer rains.
The whispers of the evening breeze,
A lullaby among the trees.

The stars emerge, a constellation,
Each twinkling light a new sensation.
In twilight's hold, our spirits sway,
As night unfolds its dark array.

Embrace the fading, let it be,
An end without a need to flee.
In every dusk, new stories start,
In fading light, we find the heart.

Chasing the Briefest Day

The sun dips low, a fleeting glow,
As shadows stretch across the way.
In twilight's dance, we chase the light,
Embracing whispers of the night.

The colors fade, yet hearts ignite,
In every breeze, a hint of play.
We gather warmth, we share our dreams,
In fragile moments, hope redeems.

With every breath, the world unwinds,
A fleeting spark, unafraid to sway.
Together, we embrace the dusk,
A gentle touch in twilight's husk.

The stars will rise, the dreams awake,
As darkness wraps the earth in gray.
So let us roam till we're embraced,
By night's soft cloak, our fears erased.

Whispering Winds of Change

The winds begin their gentle song,
A hush that stirs both land and sea.
With every gust, a story born,
Of dreams that rise and hearts set free.

Leaves flutter soft on branches bare,
They tell of paths and journeys bold.
With every shift, a chance to dare,
The air is thick with tales retold.

In swirling clouds, the future waits,
Each breath a promise, every chance.
With open hands, we greet the fates,
The winds of change invite the dance.

So let us walk where whispers guide,
With courage found in warm embrace.
The winds will lead, we shall abide,
In every step, a boundless grace.

A Time for Stillness

In quiet corners, shadows blend,
The world outside begins to fade.
We find our heartbeats, soft and slow,
In stillness, peace is gently laid.

The clock's soft ticking, muted sounds,
As moments stretch like echoes wide.
We savor breaths, the calm surrounds,
In harmony, our worries bide.

In tranquil pools, reflections play,
A canvas bare, our thoughts can flow.
We gather strength, as night gives way,
To morning's light, a softened glow.

So let us pause, embrace the hush,
In nature's calm, where dreams align.
For in the still, there's always rush,
That lets our spirits gently shine.

Beneath the Starlit Haze

With whispers soft, the night unfolds,
A tapestry of lights so bright.
We wander close beneath the stars,
In wonder caught by moon's sweet light.

The cosmos swirls, a dance divine,
In every glance, a story shared.
The constellations weave their signs,
Reminding us that hope is bared.

With every twinkle, secrets told,
In shadows deep, our dreams take flight.
We cast our wishes on the cold,
And sail our hearts on wings of night.

So let us dream, as stars align,
In stillness rich with futures embraced.
Beneath the haze, our souls entwined,
In cosmic glow, we find our place.

Lullaby of the Longest Night

Stars softly whisper, dreams take flight,
The moon is glowing, draped in white.
Crickets sing sweetly, night feels near,
Close your eyes gently, cast off the fear.

Shadows dance slowly, swaying low,
Winds sing a tale, soft and slow.
Waves in the distance, rocking the shore,
Lull you to slumber, evermore.

Blanket of darkness, wraps us tight,
Cozy and warm in the still of night.
Peace finds a moment, in the calm,
Embers of twilight, a soothing balm.

Every heartbeat, drumming serene,
Wrapped in the magic, softly unseen.
Veil of the evening, soft and deep,
Lullaby whispers, carrying dreams to sleep.

Stillness in the Turning World

Hold your breath softly, let it go,
Time weaves its fabric, gentle and slow.
Moments like shadows, fleeting and bright,
Stillness surrounds us, whispering light.

Branches sway gently, in the breeze,
Nature's sweet silence, putting us at ease.
Ripples on water, dance in repose,
Life hugs the stillness, and quietly grows.

Stars flicker softly, in endless night,
Each tiny pinprick, a shimmering sight.
Harmony hums in the soft dusk,
In the calm of the world, we find trust.

Eyes meet the heavens, hearts beat as one,
Under the watch of the patient sun.
Whispers of nature, softly embrace,
In the turning world, we find our place.

Dusk's Embrace

Golden hues fading, day takes flight,
Embers of sunlight, surrender to night.
Clouds wear their tints of purple and gray,
Dusk beckons softly, calling the day.

A hush falls around, the world slows down,
Evening's cool whisper, no need for a frown.
Stars peek from curtains, twinkling with grace,
In the arms of dusk, we find our space.

The moon starts to rise, casting a spell,
Filling the shadows with stories to tell.
Night drapes its blanket, calm and wide,
Dusk holds us gently, a comforting guide.

Silhouettes linger, under the stars,
Dreams drift like whispers, carried afar.
In dusk's warm embrace, we learn to see,
The beauty of endings, and what can be.

Solitary Light in the Dark

In the depths of night, one candle glows,
Flickering gently, amid all the woes.
A beacon of hope, in shadowy seas,
Whispers of warmth, carried by the breeze.

Eyes in the darkness, searching for peace,
Lonely hearts find strength, longing for release.
Through trials and tempests, we find our way,
Guided by light, turning night into day.

Stars twinkle keenly, offering dreams,
In the vast silence, nothing is as it seems.
A solitary lantern, holding the night,
Filling the void with soft sparkles of light.

Each gleam is a promise, a story untold,
Shining through shadows, brave and bold.
In the depths of darkness, hope shines clear,
The solitary light draws love ever near.

The Pause of Time

In whispers soft, the moments wait,
A hush descends, we contemplate.
The clock ticks slow, a gentle sigh,
Embracing stillness, we aim high.

With every breath, the world seems new,
As shadows dance in twilight's hue.
Time stretches thin, like fine spun lace,
A fleeting glimpse of sacred space.

And as we pause in silent grace,
We find our hopes in this vast place.
Each second holds a timeless thread,
In this quiet, thoughts are fed.

Herein the still, the heart can soar,
Forget the past, draw near and explore.
The pause of time, a treasure rare,
In this moment, we find our care.

A Stillness to Remember

In twilight's glow, the silence reigns,
A perfect peace in softly lain.
With every breath, the heartbeats synchronize,
A stillness whispers, a sweet reprise.

The stars begin their gentle twinkling,
As night unfurls with a soft sprinkling.
In these clear hours, we find our way,
In shadows cast, our dreams can play.

Each moment gathers, like the tide,
We stand together, hearts open wide.
The memories linger, warm and bright,
In this stillness, we hold the night.

A moment's peace, a breath to take,
In silence deep, we choose to wake.
This stillness wraps us like a thread,
In whispered truths, our hearts are led.

Moments Before the Dawn

In shadows long, the night retreats,
The world awaits, as silence beats.
A fragile light begins to rise,
Moments swirl in dusky skies.

The air is crisp, with hope anew,
In gentle tones of silver hue.
With every breath, the day unfolds,
A canvas brushed in pastel golds.

The stars grow dim, their time is done,
As darkness fades, a day begun.
We stand on edges, hearts in flight,
Just moments before the dawn's first light.

Each heartbeat echoes in this space,
With every sigh, we feel its grace.
These precious seconds, ours to claim,
In dawn's embrace, we find our name.

Wings of the Night Air

Underneath the starry skies,
The nightingale begins to rise.
With wings of dreams, they take to flight,
In whispered songs that pierce the night.

The world beneath is fast asleep,
While shadows dance and secrets keep.
With every note, the heart takes wing,
A melody the night will sing.

In quiet corners, thoughts arise,
Like fireflies in the summer skies.
They twirl and sway, so light, so free,
In the embrace of night's decree.

As time slips fast, we find our place,
In every moment, every space.
The wings of night, a fleeting grace,
In hidden realms, our hearts can chase.

A Pause in Time

In the stillness of the hour,
Moments weave like threads of light.
Whispers dance in muted power,
As day transforms into the night.

Time stands still, a quiet grace,
Each tick a heartbeat, soft and slow.
In the shadows, memories trace,
A gentle ebb, a tender flow.

Leaves flutter down to kiss the ground,
Nature sighs in moment's hold.
Here, in silence, peace is found,
A story told, a dream unfolds.

Breathe in the calm, embrace the pause,
Let worries fade like distant chime.
In this space, we find our cause,
A sweet escape, a cherished time.

As stars awaken, twinkling bright,
We find our place in starry skies.
In this pause, we feel the light,
A sacred bond that never dies.

Frosted Echoes of Twilight

Twilight cloaks the world in chill,
A frosted breath, the air turns crisp.
Whispers curl in shadows still,
As light succumbs to night's soft lisp.

Crystals form on window panes,
Nature's art, a fleeting sight.
Each breath leaves gentle, icy stains,
A fleeting dance in fading light.

The horizon glows with muted fire,
As day surrenders, bids goodbye.
In stillness, hearts begin to tire,
Underneath a vast, dark sky.

Silhouette of trees arise,
Etched against the twilight's hue.
Beneath the stars, a heart complies,
In this moment, dreams feel true.

Frosted echoes weave through night,
A soft embrace, a whispered song.
United in the absence of light,
We find where we truly belong.

The Solace of Shivering Stars

Underneath the sky so vast,
Shivering stars shine bright and clear.
Whispers of the night hold fast,
Their quiet glow, a guide so dear.

Dreams drift on the gentle breeze,
Carried forth by moonlit sighs.
In the calm, our hearts find ease,
While constellation stories rise.

Each twinkle holds a secret sound,
Inviting us to share our fears.
In their watch, we stand our ground,
And shed our sadness, our lost tears.

The night unfolds like velvet deep,
A sanctuary far from strife.
In starlit calm, we softly sleep,
Finding solace, rekindling life.

With every heartbeat, we align,
Beneath the shivering starlit art.
In their glow, our spirits shine,
Guided by the night's pure heart.

Echoing Silence of the Night

In the hush, the world transforms,
Echoes whisper through the air.
Silence wraps in softest swarms,
An embrace beyond compare.

Crickets sing a lullaby,
Notes that drift like shadows long.
In the stillness, dreams can fly,
Crafting verses, quiet song.

Moonlight glimmers on the lake,
Ripples weave a silver thread.
In this peace, our hearts awake,
To tales that innocence once fed.

Stars watch over, knowing eyes,
Witnessing the time we share.
In their gaze, we find the wise,
A memory to linger there.

With every breath, a story waits,
Echoing silence, soft and sweet.
In the dark, our fate creates,
A union where our souls can meet.

Unheard Memories

In shadows deep, whispers call,
Faded echoes of a time so small.
Images dance in the mind's embrace,
Unseen threads we cannot chase.

Lost in moments never told,
A tapestry of warmth, but cold.
Footsteps linger on dusty floors,
Hearts remember what time ignores.

The laughter fades, a silent bell,
In the corners where shadows dwell.
Each sigh a story left unspun,
Unheard memories, one by one.

They weave like dreams in the night,
Crafting tales that feel so right.
With every heartbeat, we redefine,
These echoes soft, a subtle sign.

Endless corridors of the past,
Fleeting glances, shadows cast.
In these murmurs, love still gleams,
Unveiled in our forgotten dreams.

A Tapestry of Quiet Moments

In the stillness, time unfolds,
Whispers of calm, a tale retold.
Soft sunbeams break through the haze,
A tapestry woven in gentle ways.

Every glance, a thread so fine,
Stitched together, yours and mine.
The world pauses, breath held tight,
In quiet moments, hearts take flight.

Raindrops dance on windowpanes,
Nature's lullaby, soft refrains.
With every pause, we find our peace,
In simple moments, joy does increase.

The fragrance of tea, the warmth of a smile,
Comfort in stillness, if just for a while.
Together we weave through the mundane,
A tapestry rich, where love remains.

So let us gather these threads of light,
In every shadow, find joy bright.
A tapestry crafted with memories dear,
In these quiet moments, love draws near.

Night's Solace

Under a blanket of endless sky,
Stars twinkle gently, a whispered sigh.
Moonlight bathes the world so still,
In night's embrace, we find our will.

The hush of night, a comforting cloak,
With every shadow, a soft-spoken joke.
Dreams unfurl, like petals in bloom,
Within the darkness, dispelling gloom.

Crickets play a symphony sweet,
While the heart pulses with each heartbeat.
Night whispers secrets, softly spoken,
In this solace, the silence unbroken.

Beneath the stars, we close our eyes,
Imagining worlds where eternity lies.
In this moment, we are free,
Finding peace in night's mystery.

With the dawn, shadows start to fade,
Memories linger, and dreams cascade.
Yet in the dark, our spirits soar,
Night's solace whispers forevermore.

The Dance of the Northern Sky

In twilight's grace, the sky ignites,
Colors swirl, as day takes flight.
Auroras shimmer, green and gold,
A dance of spirits, ancient and bold.

Stars twirl gracefully, hand in hand,
Lighting the dark like an endless band.
Whispers of wind carry their song,
In this moment, where dreams belong.

The northern lights embrace the night,
Painting stories in cosmic light.
Each flicker tells a tale untamed,
A symphony sung, forever named.

As shadows play, and colors blend,
The universe whispers, time to suspend.
In the cool night air, hearts unite,
In the dance of sky, lost in delight.

So let us twirl beneath this glow,
As stars guide us where we need to go.
In the northern sky, our spirits gleam,
Together we dance, together we dream.

Breath of the Year's End

Whispers of frost, the silence grows,
Leaves fall softly, as the cold wind blows.
Stars emerge, bright in the darkened sky,
Time stands still, as the moments fly.

Gathered memories, tucked away tight,
Reflections dance in the fading light.
A tale unfolds of laughter and tears,
In the quiet, we embrace our fears.

Nightfall's Gentle Touch

The moon ascends, a silver embrace,
Shadows lengthen, in the evening's grace.
Crickets sing their lullabies sweet,
As sleep drapes softly, a comforting sheet.

Stars twinkle bright in the velvet sky,
While dreams take flight, learning to fly.
The world grows calm as the day takes a rest,
In night's warm arms, we find our best.

Echoes of a Fading Sun

Golden rays flicker, gently they wane,
Casting long shadows, whispering pain.
Time drips slow, like honeyed gold,
Stories of warmth in the night unfold.

A canvas painted in hues of desire,
The sky ablaze, a heart's quiet fire.
As daylight retreats, we cherish the glow,
In echoes of dusk, our spirits grow.

Celestial Murmurs

Starlit secrets in the calm night air,
Voices of cosmos whisper everywhere.
A symphony sung in the twilight's hush,
In the stillness, we feel the rush.

Galaxies twirl in a cosmic dance,
Inviting the dreamers, offering a chance.
Underneath the heavens, hearts intertwine,
In celestial murmurings, we find our sign.

Lanterns of the Unseen

In shadows dance the lights so bright,
Whispers of hope in the silent night.
Ghosts of dreams in the gentle breeze,
Illuminate paths with delicate ease.

Flickering flames in a hidden glade,
Guide the lost where the heart is laid.
Each lantern sways with a story old,
Secrets of lives in the glow they hold.

Rain falls softly on petals fair,
Binding the earth with an ethereal care.
Lanterns sway as the world moves slow,
Revealing shades we rarely know.

Through winding paths where eagles soar,
These guiding lights weave tales of yore.
In every flicker, a promise remains,
In the unseen, love still gains.

Let us wander where the light does lead,
With every step, plant the seed.
For lanterns glow in the dark's embrace,
Showing us beauty in every place.

Candles in the Gloom

In corners dark where whispers tread,
Candles flicker, lighting dread.
Flames that dance with secrets tight,
Hold the dreams of a fateful night.

Softly melting, dripping wax,
Time slips by in gentle laps.
Each candle holds a heart's desire,
Burning bright, a silent fire.

Shadows stretch in the dim-lit room,
Echoes fade beneath the loom.
Whispers linger close to the flame,
Candles burn, yet never shame.

Watch the glow as the minutes flee,
Captured by moments that choose to be.
Hope flickers in the softest flame,
In the gloom, we'll make our name.

Let us cherish every light,
In the gloom, we find our sight.
Battles fought in the quiet hour,
With candles' warmth, we find our power.

Veils of Midnight

Under the cloak of a starry night,
Veils of darkness, a mesmerizing sight.
Silken whispers that softly unfold,
Tales of mystery in silence told.

With each breath, the night draws near,
Embracing secrets, holding dear.
Shadows entwine where the dreams take flight,
Beneath the magic of moon's soft light.

A dance begins where the stars align,
Veils of midnight, a secret design.
Glimmers hidden in twilight's hue,
Offering glimpses of all that's true.

Lost in the depths of the evening's gaze,
Navigating through a silvery maze.
Veils whisper soft, guiding the way,
Carrying hopes that drift and sway.

As dawn approaches, the veils will part,
Revealing the tales that warm the heart.
In midnight's embrace, we forever dwell,
For in silence, deep stories dwell.

Reflection of Celestial Dreams

In dreams we soar through the night's embrace,
Stars reflect in the starlit space.
Celestial whispers guide the way,
Every heartbeat in cosmic sway.

Galaxies swirl in a dance divine,
Each twinkle sparkles with tales enshrined.
In the realm where wishes gleam,
We wander through celestial dream.

The moonlight spills on a tranquil sea,
Carrying secrets, wild and free.
Reflections shimmer on waves so bright,
Dancing in the soft twilight.

In the stillness, we find our flight,
Cherishing peace on this moonlit night.
The universe sings in a timeless tune,
Drawing our hearts to the silver moon.

So hold the dreams in tender grace,
Let them linger, let them trace.
For in our sleep, we find the gleam,
Of life's sweet, celestial dream.

The Still Heart of Winter

Snowflakes fall without a sound,
Blanketing the frozen ground.
Breathe in the crisp, cold air,
A quiet peace, beyond compare.

Branches bare, in slumber deep,
Nature rests in tranquil sleep.
The world seems wrapped in white,
Silent whispers in the night.

Echoes in the Stillness

In the hushed and frosty dawn,
Footsteps leave the fields withdrawn.
Whispers dance through frosty trees,
Carried gently on the breeze.

Shadows linger, soft and slow,
Where the quiet rivers flow.
Echoes of a world at rest,
Nature at its very best.

Luminous Calm of the Night

Stars like jewels in velvet skies,
Moonlight glimmers, softly lies.
The world wrapped in a silken shawl,
Nighttime's beauty does enthrall.

Whispers float on cool night air,
Secrets held with tender care.
All is still, the heart takes flight,
In the luminous calm of night.

Tranquil Waters Under Ice

Still waters mirror the pale sky,
Layers of ice, the world a sigh.
Ripples fade beneath the cold,
A story of nature quietly told.

In frozen depths, a silence keeps,
Where dreams lie as the world sleeps.
A gentle hush, all is confined,
In tranquil waters, peace we find.

Light's Gentle Retreat

As daylight fades to softest hue,
The shadows stretch, the night takes cue.
Whispers of dusk in colors blend,
As day and night, their pathways lend.

The stars peek through, a timid smile,
Illuminating the Earth's long miles.
Moonlight dances on silken streams,
Carrying secrets, wishful dreams.

The sun bows low, with grace it yields,
To twilight's kiss on golden fields.
Crickets sing their evening song,
To nature's rhythm, we belong.

Soft darkness wraps the world in peace,
A gentle touch that brings release.
In light's retreat, we find our place,
Embraced by night's warm, tender grace.

The Hushed Embrace of Winter

Snowflakes whisper as they fall,
Blanketing the earth, a soft shawl.
The trees stand tall in quiet grace,
Their branches wear a shimmering lace.

Breath fogs the air, a moment brief,
In winter's hush, we find relief.
The world transformed, stark and bright,
In cold embrace, the heart ignites.

Fires crackle, warmth and glow,
As outside the winds keen and blow.
Hot cocoa sipped in cozy nooks,
Seasoned stories in our books.

Footprints traced in glimmering frost,
In winter's grip, we find what's lost.
A season of peace, serene and still,
The hush of nature, a gentle thrill.

Silence Beneath the Stars

The night unveils a velvet sky,
Where countless stars begin to vie.
In silence deep, this cosmic dance,
Invites our hearts to take a chance.

Each twinkle holds an ancient tale,
Of distant worlds where beings sail.
A hush descends, a tranquil sway,
In twilight's hold, we drift away.

Beneath the moon's soft silver gaze,
Time stands still in this quiet phase.
Voices fade to a murmur low,
As the universe begins to flow.

So let us sit and simply be,
With starlight wrapped around you and me.
In silence found beneath the glow,
The mysteries of night will show.

Chilling Serenity

A breath of cold seeps through the trees,
Winter's touch whispers in the breeze.
With frost adorned, the world takes pause,
In chilling peace, we find our cause.

The lake lies still like a polished stone,
Reflecting skies, a world alone.
Mountains dressed in glistening white,
Guard secrets of the starry night.

Footsteps crunch on the frozen ground,
Nature's heartbeat softly found.
In every flake, a crystal dream,
Of winter's art, a silvery theme.

With every breath, a frosty mist,
In tranquil moments, we persist.
Embracing chill with hearts so warm,
In winter's sway, we weather the storm.

A Solstice Reverie

Beneath the vast and shining sky,
The sun lingers, time slips by.
Shadows stretch, the day is long,
Nature hums a golden song.

Whispers of the woods arise,
Dancing leaves, the winds surprise.
Moments weave like threads of gold,
In this warmth, our hearts unfold.

As dusk descends, the glow remains,
Painting hues on window panes.
Lost in dreams of summer's light,
A solstice night, pure and bright.

Through twilight's calm, our spirits soar,
Gathering tales from days of yore.
Every heartbeat, a tender call,
In this magic, we are all.

With starlit skies that whisper low,
Moonlit paths where lovers go.
In the reverie, we abide,
Souls entwined, forever tied.

Midsummer's Secrets

In the woods where shadows play,
Midsummer's secrets softly sway.
Ferns unfurl, the blossoms bloom,
Nature hums in sweet perfume.

Crickets sing a soothing tune,
Beneath the watchful eye of moon.
Night embraces warm and bright,
Revealing all, 'neath silver light.

The fireflies weave a radiant dance,
In the darkness, they take their chance.
Whispers float on gentle air,
Magic lives, unnoticed, rare.

Paths of dreams, in twilight's glow,
Secrets linger, ever slow.
Veils of time begin to part,
Midsummer's charm enchants the heart.

As dawn awakes, the earth will sigh,
In the warmth where memories lie.
Forever held in nature's keep,
Midsummer's secrets, soft and deep.

Tranquil Transitions

The day departs with gentle hands,
While evening wraps the quiet lands.
Colors blend in soft embrace,
Tranquil moments, time slowed pace.

Birds retreat to hidden nests,
While twilight cradles day to rest.
Shadows deepen, stars ignite,
A tapestry of velvet night.

Breezes sigh a whispered tune,
Underneath the watchful moon.
Nature holds her breath, at peace,
In this stillness, worries cease.

The world transforms, a sacred space,
As light recedes, we find our grace.
Through the dusk, our spirits glide,
In tranquil transitions, we abide.

From day to night, we weave and flow,
Embracing cycles, we learn to grow.
In these moments, we find our way,
Through tranquil transitions, we stay.

Gathering Silence

In the stillness of the night,
Echoes fade, in soft moonlight.
Stars above begin to gleam,
We gather silence, a sacred dream.

Whispers float on calmest breeze,
Carrying tales among the trees.
Heartbeats merge with nature's song,
In this peace, we all belong.

Time stands still, like water's flow,
Gentle moments, sweet and slow.
From worries past, our minds release,
In gathering silence, we find peace.

Reflections dance in darkened pools,
Mirroring life's unwritten rules.
With every breath, we come alive,
In gathered silence, we thrive.

So let the world fade far away,
In this stillness, here we stay.
Finding solace in the night,
Gathering silence, pure delight.

Celestial Stillness

In the night, stars softly gleam,
Moonlit whispers weave a dream.
Silent shadows dance so light,
Wrapped in the embrace of night.

Gentle winds whisper on,
Carrying echoes from the dawn.
Stillness reigns in heavens high,
As the world quietly sighs.

Time suspends in silver rays,
Lost in the night's calm embrace.
Each heartbeat a tender pause,
In the silence, we find cause.

Beneath the vast, eternal dome,
We search for peace within our home.
Through the quiet, stars bestow,
Celestial truths we long to know.

In this space where starlight flows,
Hearts unveiled, the stillness grows.
Amidst the night, we gently stand,
In the celestial's tender hand.

Secrets of the Bosque

In whispered leaves, secrets hide,
Through ancient roots, trails collide.
A hush resides among the trees,
Breath of nature through the breeze.

Sunlight dances on the brook,
Mysteries ripe, if you look.
Echoes of the past remain,
Stories linger in the rain.

Mossy paths lead us away,
To where shadows softly play.
In this haven, time is lost,
For nature counts not the cost.

Deeper still, the heart beats strong,
An unbroken, timeless song.
Every rustle, every call,
Carries whispers, secrets all.

In the bosques, wisdom flows,
Teaching us what nature knows.
Through the leaves and tranquil air,
We find solace, free from care.

The Weight of the Still Air

In the quiet, time stands still,
Heavy hearts with dreams to fill.
Every breath a measured sigh,
Where shadows linger, softly lie.

The sun's gaze hangs low and soft,
Fingers of warmth as it aloft.
In the silence, silence speaks,
Gentle answers to our seeks.

Veils of wisps float through the calm,
Nature wraps us like a balm.
Each moment lingers, dense and sweet,
As echoes of time retreat.

We breathe in the heavy peace,
As the world begins to cease.
In this embrace, we yearn for flight,
Yet savor the weight of night.

Every whisper in the air,
Weaving spells beyond compare.
In stillness, we find our core,
As the night opens its door.

Enchanted Tenebrae

In shadows deep, enchantments weave,
A tapestry that we believe.
Midnight musings softly bloom,
Whispers linger, dispelling gloom.

Stars ignite the velvet sky,
Dancing secrets, passing by.
Ethereal forms drift with grace,
In the darkness, we find our place.

Cool night air, a lover's kiss,
Lost in dreams, a fleeting bliss.
Through tenebrae, shadows call,
Lost in wonder, we enthrall.

Each heartbeat echoes, soft and low,
As we tread where night winds blow.
In this place where magic thrives,
We discover how it survives.

Awakened, we embrace the night,
In the depths where spirits light.
Enchanted paths lead us through,
In tenebrae, we'll start anew.

Nights Wrapped in Stillness

The stars blink softly in the night,
As the world slips into dream's delight.
A hush envelops all around,
In the twilight, peace is found.

The air is crisp, a gentle chill,
Moonbeams dance on the windowsill.
Whispers of secrets softly glean,
Wrapped in the stillness, serene and clean.

Silvery shadows play their game,
Each curve and contour speaks the same.
Night's tender touch embraces tight,
Enfolded in this tranquil night.

A heart beats slow, a time for rest,
In the calm, we feel our best.
Close your eyes, let calm unwind,
In nights wrapped in stillness, peace you'll find.

With memories etched in silver light,
Dreams take flight, soaring high and bright.
Each moment lingers, soft and sweet,
In the stillness, our souls meet.

Whispering Pines and Shadows

Under the canopy, shadows play,
Whispering pines sway and sway.
Nature's breath, a gentle sigh,
In the twilight, secrets lie.

Branches sigh in the night's embrace,
Each whisper tells of a hidden place.
Moonlight filters through each seam,
Painting a soft, ethereal dream.

Soft moss cushions the earth below,
Where ancient trees, wisdom bestow.
Silence holds an age-old grace,
In this haven, time finds its pace.

The scent of pine lingers sweet,
As soft shadows dance to nature's beat.
Every rustle, a song anew,
In the night, the world feels true.

Stars peek through leaves overhead,
Guiding the weary home to bed.
With whispers soft, the pines confide,
In shadows deep, the heart can hide.

The Softness of Cold

Winter's breath, a gentle chill,
Blankets the earth, soft as a pill.
Cotton clouds drift high and low,
Each flake whispers tales of snow.

Frosted panes like lace adorn,
Mornings bright, yet lightly worn.
The softest hues, gray and white,
Bathe the world in muted light.

Bare branches etch the sky's delight,
In their stillness, they hold tight.
The cold wraps close, so tenderly,
In nature's arms, we're wild and free.

Embers glow in fireside's keep,
While outside, the world falls asleep.
With every breath, clouds rise and fold,
Capturing the softness of cold.

In the hush of winter's song,
We find the place where we belong.
Wrapped in warmth, as cold winds blow,
We cherish the soft and serene snow.

Moonlight on Winter's Edge

A silver glow on snow-draped hills,
The night awakens, the quiet thrills.
Moonlight glimmers, crystal bright,
Painting shadows in the night.

The world adorned in icy lace,
Each flake a story, every trace.
Whispers echo through the trees,
In the stillness, a gentle breeze.

Footprints crunch on paths once pure,
In moonlit realms, we feel secure.
The cold bites deep, yet hearts are warm,
Embracing the chill, a winter's charm.

Stars twinkle like a distant flame,
Each one, a dream, or a sweet name.
In the velvet sky, they weave,
A tapestry of night to believe.

As we wander through the glen,
Moonlight guides us once again.
On winter's edge, we dance and sway,
In the beauty of the night, we stay.

Breath of the Winter Solstice

Whispers of winter chill the air,
Silent nights, a frosty affair.
Stars twinkle in a velvet dome,
As the world wraps in a glistening chrome.

Time pauses in this tranquil bliss,
Where every moment holds a kiss.
The moonlight dances on frozen lakes,
In the stillness, the heart awakes.

Branches heavy with crystalline dress,
Nature's beauty, an artful caress.
The fire crackles, embers glow bright,
As shadows cloak the deepening night.

Inhale the magic, exhale the cold,
By winter's breath, our stories unfold.
Together we gather, a circle of warmth,
In the heart of the season, our spirits are sworn.

So, let the solstice draw us near,
Through whispered wishes, and festive cheer.
We celebrate life in its purest form,
As we find solace in the winter storm.

A Song for the Fading Light

As the sun dips low, colors blend,
A serenade for day's quiet end.
The sky ignites with fiery hues,
Crafting a canvas, nature's muse.

Gentle breezes hum a soft tune,
While shadows elongate, beneath the moon.
Cicadas sing their twilight song,
A soothing rhythm, where we belong.

Echoes of laughter drift through the trees,
Carried along by the whispering breeze.
In this fleeting hour, moments stand still,
As dusk captivates with mysterious thrill.

Our hearts remember, as light fades away,
All the stories woven in the day.
With each heartbeat, a memory flows,
In the arms of twilight, where love only grows.

So let the last light softly depart,
And carry with it the dreams of the heart.
For in the fading, there's beauty untold,
In each whispered promise of night's gentle hold.

Twilight's Gentle Surrender

Silhouettes stretch along the ground,
In twilight's arms, peace can be found.
The horizon blushes, kissed by the night,
As stars awaken, twinkling bright.

Soft shadows gather, the world takes a pause,
Nature exhaling, as if it just was.
Crickets chirp in the growing dark,
Their melodic whispers, a tender spark.

With every breath, the day softly fades,
In twilight's embrace, our worries abate.
The evening unfolds like a cherished dream,
Where life meanders in a gentle stream.

Time drips slowly, like honey on bread,
As fantasies linger, where worries once tread.
With the glow of the moon, our souls find their way,
In the heart of the dusk, we're meant to stay.

So let us linger as the colors dissolve,
In twilight's magic, our hearts resolve.
As the night beckons with whispers anew,
In the silence, we find what is true.

Beneath the Blanket of Snow

Softly it falls, a quiet embrace,
Covering the world in delicate lace.
Each flake a whisper, unique in its flight,
Transforming the day into shimmering white.

Beneath the blanket, life slumbers away,
In dreams of spring, where shadows won't stay.
The trees stand tall, draped in their gowns,
Guardians of secrets in snowy crowns.

Footprints imprinted on the glistening floor,
Every step echoes a tale of yore.
In the frosty silence, wonders arise,
As nature breathes beneath the gray skies.

The world holds its breath, in stillness it gleams,
Wrapped in serenity, it fosters our dreams.
With each swirling flake, we're woven anew,
In the gentle embrace, we begin to renew.

So let us cherish this moment of peace,
In the heart of the winter, our worries can cease.
For beneath the blanket, love blooms and grows,
In the quiet moments, beneath the soft snow.

The Hush of Deepest Winter

Snowflakes fall in gentle grace,
Covering the world in lace.
Branches bare, they softly sigh,
Underneath the slate-gray sky.

The air is crisp, the silence deep,
Like a secret the forest keeps.
Frosty breath, like whispered dreams,
In the stillness, nothing screams.

Icicles dangle, sharp and bright,
Catching sparkles, catching light.
Footsteps crunch on frozen ground,
In this hush, pure peace is found.

Nature sleeps, wrapped up tight,
Beneath stars, in deep, quiet night.
Time seems slow; the world stands still,
In winter's grasp, there's warmth to fill.

In the hush of deepest chill,
Hearts are calm and spirits thrill.
Wrapped in layers, we draw near,
Finding comfort in what we hold dear.

Luminescent Quietude

The moon spills silver on the lake,
Ripples dance, awake, awake.
Stars surround in twinkling grace,
A celestial, vast embrace.

Softly hums the evening breeze,
Carrying secrets through the trees.
Gentle whispers of the night,
Wrap the world in softest light.

Each shadow holds a silent tale,
In twilight's glow, we set sail.
Into dreams, our thoughts take flight,
In luminescent quiet night.

Crickets sing a lullaby,
As constellations fill the sky.
In the calm, our spirits mend,
Trusting in the night to lend.

Together we find solace here,
In quietude, we shed our fear.
With hearts aglow in gentle love,
We embrace the stars above.

Dreaming Under the Still Sky

Beneath a canopy of deep blue,
We lie in fields where wildflowers grew.
Softly swaying, the grass does sigh,
As we weave our dreams up high.

Clouds drift by like thoughts untold,
In the warmth, we feel bold.
With each breath, beneath the vast,
We find ourselves, our burdens past.

The golden sun begins to fade,
Painting hues, the evening's blade.
A gentle breeze, a soothing balm,
In this moment, we are calm.

Stars emerge as daylight wanes,
Each a story, spark, and chain.
We gather wishes, let them fly,
Dreaming under the still sky.

A quiet promise, a shared delight,
With twilight wrapping us so tight.
In the night, we'll stay entwined,
In dreams more brilliant than we've designed.

Whispers of the Solstice

The longest night begins to speak,
In shadows deep, our hearts grow weak.
Yet in the dark, a spark ignites,
With every whisper, hope takes flight.

Nature pauses, holding breath,
In the stillness, we confront death.
Yet warmth emerges from within,
As the cycle starts again.

Candles flicker, soft and bright,
Guiding us through this longest night.
Gathered close, we tell our tales,
Of love, of life, as courage pales.

The solstice calls; we heed the sound,
In darkness, unity is found.
From this moment, we arise,
Carrying dreams to greet the skies.

With each dawn, a promise blooms,
Chasing away the winter's glooms.
Whispers linger, softly ring,
As we prepare for the joys that spring.

The Veil of Hushed Dreams

In the stillness of the night,
Whispers dance in gentle flight.
Stars twinkle softly up above,
Cradling secrets wrapped in love.

Shadows play on moonlit streams,
Holding close our tender dreams.
Each heartbeat sings a quiet tune,
Beneath the watchful, silvery moon.

A velvet cloak, the world asleep,
In thoughts so deep, we softly creep.
Through the mist, our wishes glide,
In the realm where hopes abide.

The breeze carries an ancient song,
A lullaby where we belong.
In every sigh, a wish is cast,
As we wander, free at last.

With every shade that drifts away,
The dawn will break, a brand-new day.
But in the night, we find our space,
Enveloped in this dreamlike grace.

Reflections in the Frost

Morning light on frosted glass,
Nature's art as moments pass.
Each crystal shines a fleeting spark,
Etched in time, a tale so stark.

Whispers of the chill in air,
Each breath a fog, a tender prayer.
Footprints marked on glittered ground,
In silence, beauty can be found.

Brittle leaves that softly fall,
Under the weight of winter's call.
Glistening branches, nature's crown,
Waking dreams from slumber down.

Reflections dance in sparkled light,
Painting landscapes, pure and bright.
A canvas bright with winter's cheer,
In stillness found, the world is clear.

As shadows lengthen, day departs,
Frosty wonders fill our hearts.
In every corner, brilliance grows,
A fleeting glimpse, forever flows.

Solace in the Darkened Hours

When day succumbs to velvet night,
Stars emerge, a guiding light.
In shadows deep, our worries fade,
In whispered breaths, our fears are laid.

A quiet calm, the world at rest,
In darkness, we are truly blessed.
Softly falls the silver glow,
Illuminating paths we know.

Hushed voices carry through the air,
As if the night invites a prayer.
Wrapped in dreams, we gently sway,
In this embrace, we long to stay.

The hours linger, time slows down,
As starlit veils our hearts surround.
In each moment, peace we find,
A refuge for both soul and mind.

So let the night weave tales anew,
In shadows soft, our spirits grew.
With every heartbeat, solace calls,
In darkened hours, love never falls.

The Lullaby of Winter's Chill

Snowflakes dance on chilly air,
Each one a dream, floating with care.
They blanket earth in soft embrace,
Whispers of peace in winter's face.

A hush descends, the world so still,
Nature sleeps, a tranquil thrill.
Fires crackle with warming light,
As shadows waltz into the night.

The pine trees wear their coats of white,
Guardians of the tranquil night.
Beneath their boughs, we find our peace,
In winter's kiss, our worries cease.

The moon shines bright, a sentinel,
Listening close to every swell.
In starlit dreams, our hearts unite,
Bound together by soft twilight.

So let us rest, embrace the chill,
In winter's arms, our hearts shall fill.
With each embrace, a soothing thrill,
To the lullaby of winter's chill.

Between Day and Night

Shadows stretch as sun sinks low,
Colors blend in twilight's glow.
Whispers dance on evening's breath,
Life's sweet balance, love and death.

Stars awaken, soft and bright,
Painting dreams in soft twilight.
The moon casts silver on the land,
A quiet magic, softly planned.

Birds find rest, their songs now cease,
Nature settles into peace.
A gentle hush wraps round the day,
As light and dark begin to play.

Fading warmth and cooler air,
Hints of dreams begin to stir.
Within the space of dusk's embrace,
We find our calm, our sacred place.

Between the realms of day and night,
Hope shines softly, pure and bright.
In this moment, fears take flight,
For all is well between the light.

Celestial Stillness

In the depths of velvet skies,
Stars hold secrets, silent cries.
Galaxies in quiet flight,
Whisper tales of ancient light.

Comets streak with fiery grace,
Painting dreams in endless space.
Planets spin in cosmic dance,
In the stillness, round we prance.

Nebulae in colors bloom,
Breath of life amidst the gloom.
Moonbeams weave a silver thread,
Guiding souls in dreams unsaid.

As the night wraps all around,
Every heartbeat, every sound.
In this vast, celestial sea,
We find our place, we find the key.

Stillness reigns, yet pulses life,
In the calm beyond the strife.
Reach for stars, hold on so tight,
In the dark, we seek the light.

Fireflies at Dusk

Among the shadows, soft and sweet,
Fireflies dance on tiny feet.
Twinkling lights in evening's veil,
A fleeting glimpse, a whispered tale.

They flicker bright, like hope reborn,
Guiding hearts through dusk's soft scorn.
A magical ballet of light,
Chasing dreams into the night.

Children laugh, with jars in hand,
Chasing sparks across the land.
Nature's gems, they rise and fall,
A symphony, enchanting all.

In the air, a fragrant breeze,
Rustling softly through the trees.
Each firefly, a fleeting spark,
Illuminating friendly dark.

As darkness drapes the world in peace,
In their glow, our cares release.
Fleeting moments, joy ignites,
In fireflies that grace the nights.

Embracing the Night's Lull

Softly now, the night descends,
With gentle hands, the day it bends.
Whispers of the stars above,
Cradle dreams wrapped in love.

Moonlight spills on glassy lakes,
Silence sings, the heart awakes.
Floating beams of silver glow,
Guide us where the emotions flow.

Crickets chirp their evening song,
Nature's chorus, deep and strong.
In the stillness, hearts expand,
In this realm, we take a stand.

Close your eyes, let worries fade,
In this moment, unafraid.
Embrace the night, its soothing call,
In the lull, we find it all.

As stars twinkle and shadows play,
Rest your thoughts at the end of day.
In the quiet, let love swell,
In the night, all is well.

www.ingramcontent.com/pod-product-compliance
Ingram Content Group UK Ltd.
Pitfield, Milton Keynes, MK11 3LW, UK
UKHW031945151224
452382UK00006B/103